INTERLUDES

PRAYERS
OF
REMEMBRANCE

INTERLUDES

PRAYERS
OF
REMEMBRANCE

FREDERICK W. KEMPER

Publishing House
St. Louis

INTERLUDES

Library of Congress Cataloging in Publication Data

Kemper, Frederick, W
    Interludes.

        1. Devotional exercises. I. Title.
BV4832.2.K42   242'.3   78-13495
ISBN 0-570-03786-7

Contents

Foreword

Except for the garbage man's wife, who ever prays for him? To some our Lord has given the gift of making us laugh. Say a prayer of thanksgiving for them, say I. Then there is the poor dentist—whoever prays for him? We're more likely to pray for ourselves in the waiting room. Can you imagine the preacher standing at the high altar praying about the human gene pool or human guinea pigs?

It struck me one day that all the prayers in all the books I had on prayer (except those that tried to be cute) missed some people and things that needed praying for. Some people and some things only needed a word of thanks said about them—like sunsets and mountains. On the other hand there was an enormous number of unnoticed objects for prayer out there. So this little book came to be written.

The object of these devotions is not to convert anybody, or to strengthen anyone in the faith, or to encourage anyone to a better or more dedicated life. It unabashedly wants to bring to visibility the unprayed for, and to suggest a little prayer for the moment, to that end.

These little devotions were first used as an interlude in the morning worship. For a number of weeks hand running somebody was asking for church time—the youth, the Red Cross, the candy makers, mothers. Most preachers, I hope, have an aversion to using pulpit time for most "weeks," as important as they may be. The two ideas cohesed into a two-minute slot toward the end of the service and into a hymn, a brief note, and a "Collect for Mother." When the requests ran low the other prayers gave the interlude idea continuity and kept the habit available until further requests were made.

Remembrances of this kind may be incorporated into the liturgy within the framework of the general prayer under the reference "for all sorts and conditions of men." If there is time an appropriate hymn may be used to introduce the interlude. Suggestions for such are found at the beginning of each interlude, and sources for the hymns are listed at the end of this booklet. Hymn texts not found in the hymnal of your church may be inserted in the bulletin, taking care to obtain permission to do so for hymns not in the public domain—or other appropriate available hymn stanzas may be substituted in their place.

These "devotions" hardly have to be used in church. Whatever is to stop a family in devotion from praying for heretics or optimists or commuters? Besides, the various ideas might invite discussion about ethics and morals, kindness and caring, right there at the family dinner table.

Here they are. With them goes the hope that they stir up a host of other possibilities. There is no end to the people and the gifts of a gracious God for which we might pause and say our thanks. Nor does there seem to be an end to the problems that find resolution through prayer. Even the Gethsemane angel was an answer to a prayer, and in that instance the answer was a flat no. Pray anyway; how else can you be in communication with God?

Has Anybody Seen Integrity?

**(Hymn: "Where Cross the Crowded Ways of Life")
Frank M. North**

This is certain: the news media, all of them, bring tons of bad news into our homes every day for us. We live through corrupt premiers, shahs, presidents, governors, senators, congressmen, etc. Every day brings news of wars, protests, minority oppression, not to mention robbery, assault, rape, and the new morality. If a person hasn't got the ability to shrug off the negative, he'd best stay away from the news. Humanity comes off rather disgracefully, if it must be judged by what the media reports of it.

If one is not careful he might easily begin to wonder whatever happened to chivalry, honor, self-denial, and integrity. Where, he might ask, are the restraints that kept rein on greed, pride, and lust? Is it because God is dead—in too many people? Is it perhaps because the moral law has been scrapped in favor of self-indulgence? Whatever it is, it has left men and nations without that virtue called integrity—a virtue badly needed in our time. Without it, how can faith in people, in leaders, and in nations be maintained?

A Collect for Integrity

Divine Creator, You have "made of one blood all nations of men for to dwell on all the face of the earth" (KJV). Set all people's vision distant enough to see You. Then, whether trembling before Your justice or drawing strength from Your mercy, set them to living as trustworthy and trusting servants to each other in this shrinking 20th-century cottage we call earth; through Jesus Christ, Your Son, our Lord, with whom You and the Holy Spirit are one God, with dominion over us forever. Amen.

For the Beauty Created by Man's Hand

(Hymn: "For the Beauty of the Earth")
Folliott S. Pierpont

Beauty started with God—and how generous He was with it! The blue vault of sky was His idea. He filled the vault with everchanging moods by adding clouds, sun rays on clouds, and storms. He put the birds free-soaring in the heavens. He thrust the mountains up high against the sky. He planted the first flowers on the forest floor. He devised the snowflake, the snowfall, and the snow blanket. God is obviously a lover of the beautiful. He went to great lengths to supply us with an endless amount of it.

Man cannot match what God has done, but he does glorious things nonetheless. The bounding gazelles in splendid color on cave walls are a superb exhibit of man's sense of rhythm in simple lines. The majestic columns in an Egyptian temple, the soaring arches in a Gothic cathedral, the rich ceramic tile of the Persians, the marble shaped by medieval chisels, and canvases painted by modern impressionists bear symbolic and eloquent testimony to the ability of man to use the artistic talents he bears in the image of God. Beauty does not belong to the great alone. The floral arrangement on a dining table, the patchwork quilt handed down from Grandma, and a homemade cake are as beautiful in their own way as the work of the master, for they are the investment of a talent, too.

A Collect for Artists

For the need planted in most of us for things beautiful, and for the artistic skill imparted to some among us to do them—O great God, who made us all, accept our rendered praise and gratitude for the artists and their art, for they bring joy, excitement and wonder into our lives; through Jesus Christ, Your Son, our Lord, with whom You and the Holy Spirit are one God, with dominion over us forever. Amen.

Violators and Victims

(Hymn: "Day of Wrath, O Day of Mourning")
Thomas de Celano

Rats in an overcrowded controlled situation are observed to behave abnormally. Their normal habit patterns give way to meanness, violence, and sexual perversion (even for rats). Most animals seem to need their own little piece of turf to survive and live in a normal way.

Man does, too. But man has a thousand pressures the rat doesn't have (although the rat obviously has its own, even when conditions are normal). Man's ability to think, rationalize, and moralize should give him a great edge beyond any animal. Yet it is possible to stifle conscience, to rationalize on either end of a 180° spectrum, and to think in any direction on a 360° arc. All this does not excuse, it only explains that it is possible for man to do the horrible things he does. Blame some of it on genes, some of it on environment, all of it on the Old Adam in us and the Christ out of us, by our own design.

The recent death of a little girl poised at the edge of her adulthood is overwhelmingly awful. Young men, with potential for sainthood, lured her to an isolated spot, used her, abused her, and murdered her. The result of that moment no one but the participants saw. But the event leaves one body, a number of damaged lives, a family whose tears will never end, a neighborhood that must live with terror, and thousands of outraged citizens. The victim is only one of untold numbers of molested, mutilated, murdered children (and adults).

Civil law comes too late except to avenge. Moral law, that might have stopped such things, was violated. The laws of love and concern were probably unknown and could not be applied. While families mourn and neighbors

12

tremble, a conscienceless, sensual, violent person is tried, maybe sentenced, maybe freed in the labyrinth of legal threads, but either way he is a person with a horrible past. Is one granite stone and a vase of wilted gladioli monument enough for either violator or victim?

A Collect for "Violators"

Righteous God, whose moral code allows no deviation with judgment and whose love lifts the penitent and believing sinner, deal righteously and mercifully with men (and women) who molest, abuse, and often murder others. Keep us from reciprocal and unrestrained violence, lest we be guilty in kind as we deal with such people among us according to our civil laws; through Jesus Christ, Your Son, our Lord, with whom You and the Holy Spirit are one God, with dominion over us forever. Amen.

A Collect for a Victim's Relatives and Friends

Great God, whose arms are strong and whose heart is love, sustain those whose broken hearts need healing and whose footsteps are unsure because great sorrow stalks their lives, for they live in the darkness of not knowing and in the unfathomable mystery of Your divine will and purpose; through Jesus Christ, Your Son, our Lord, with whom You and the Holy Spirit are one God, with dominion over us forever. Amen.

A Collect for Our Security

We recognize the endless dangers in this world in which we live, Heavenly Father, whose eye is ever on the sparrow, and ask Your divine protection, lest we become victims of other men's violence, or ourselves become violators; through Jesus Christ, Your Son, our Lord, with whom You and the Holy Spirit are one God, with dominion over us forever. Amen.

Thank God for Heretics

(Hymn: "Thy Hand, O God, Has Guided")
Edward Hayes Plumptre

The bones of "heretics" lie strewn along the rocky road of the church visible. If deviating from the standards of the institution or the power party makes heretics, there have been legions of them. Many of them are only a hairline away from being reformers. Certainly a great many of the old bones littering the church's history ought to be picked up and given a decent burial. All the rest ought to be picked up and blessed. Not all heretics were/are bad to the point of deserving banishment or death.

All heretics made contribution to the church, whether in or out of it. Every time one of them presented his point of view (his heresy), the church was forced, or should have been, to reexamine its position. If the church had not reexamined itself the heretic might have been right and then who would have been heretic? Or if on examination the church finds no fault with itself, it might be heretic against the standards of the Spirit.

The list of heretics/reformers is long and impressive. Consider such names as Athanasius, Savonarola, Hus, Luther, Calvin, Pope John XXIII. Some need exhuming and reburial in the family crypt; the names on the obverse list can quietly be removed from the sacred crypt and given respectful burial in the potter's field. Epitaphs in the crypt should read, "Reformer, he changed directions." Scratch on the board that marks the grave of the deviate who was wrong, "He made us think; God rest his soul."

A Collect for Heretics

Holy Spirit, Lord of the church, give Your church an ample supply of "heretics" to keep her searching for truth, and save both church and heretic from heresy, lest the road they travel be dead end; through Jesus Christ, our Lord, to whom the church is Bride and with whom You and the Father are one God, with dominion over us forever. Amen.

Help! It's a Complex World

(Hymn: "Lead Me, Lord")
Samuel S. Wesley

Moving from womb to tomb has never been an easy process for God's people. It is safe to assert that our world has all the old temptations and a passel of new ones beside. The old censure and its restraints are gone. The shade is up and the window is open. Before Hegel most things were black or white, right or wrong. Hegel added the third possibility when he allowed for "gray" and "maybe" in the open and shut world. The Hegelian discovery became a watershed in philosophy. It opened the door for an "anything goes, nothing is sacred" way of life.

We have reaped the whirlwind in our time and culture of a hedonistic blast that has left ethics and morals a shambles. Life has no meaning and God is dead! Drink a toast to freedom. Have another to the new me. We've managed to slip the tether and the sky's the limit. Pandora's box is full of pleasures and they didn't tell us.

Peers tell exciting stories of their economic prowess. Their "dress code" is dictated by the Old Adam in us. Their novels are lurid, their magazines are reprobate, their entertainment is explicit. Their biological conquests are common knowledge. All the while there is no thunder in the distance, no visible retribution. God is in His heavens—or dead—and the world is all right.

And God's humble person, remembering the cross and squinting for a glimpse of the Throne, struggles with the old nature that just won't leave and the new creature he/she is in Jesus Christ. Enticement comes again and again. The temptation to be less than he/she wants to be in Christ is constant. The high commitment must be shored up time after time, for the deed cannot be less than the creed.

A Collect for Guidance in Our World

Guide us, Holy Spirit, eternal Light, through the dark, labyrinthian paths from which we must pick our way in this complex world, lest we lose our way and displease You and harm ourselves; through Jesus Christ, our Lord, with whom You and the Father are one God, with dominion over us forever. Amen.

Memorial Day

(Hymn: "Not Alone for Mighty Empire")
William P. Merrill

It is a great blessing and comfort to live in a country with a good history. Not everything we keep in our archives can stand the bright sunlight. The saga of the American Indian has many embarrassing episodes in it. We have a few wars we'd like to preserve under lock and key in the dark cellar. Most of the negative events of our history have been positively resolved.

America was born in the pangs of tyranny and oppression. She was weaned on a revolutionary war. Her growing pains include the great sickness of a civil war, and, after that, other wars of varying intensity, each with its noble ideals and its price—in hurt and sorrow and death. It is because the price of freedom, unity and high ideals must be paid in the sacrifice of limb and life that a day to remember exists. "To you with failing hands we throw the torch. Be yours to hold it high!" a soldier-poet wrote when the guns of World War I were at last silent. We remember and honor those whose lifeblood secured our homeland.

Remembering and honoring those who had made the sacrifice is the lesser half of the memorial. An endless concern for peace in the great brotherhood of mankind is the other. "If ye break faith with us who die, we shall not rest . . . in Flanders Field," or in a hundred other gardens around the world where the Star of David and the Cross of Christ are tended by a grateful country.

A Collect for Memorial Day

Lord God Omnipotent, whose Son lived and died to bring peace on earth, whose desire is for plowshares made of Damascus steel and mighty lions friendly to defenseless lambs, we confess that we have frustrated Your hopes and smashed Your dreams; yet we are grateful for and honor the heroes of our land who have sacrificed time and limb and life for peace, and we pray that we may hold Your dream as ours and with Your blessing expend ourselves in striving for it; through Jesus Christ, Your Son, our Lord, with whom You and the Holy Spirit are one God, with dominion over us forever. Amen.

The Militant Church
(Civil War)

(Hymn: "Jesus, with Thy Church Abide")
Thomas B. Pollock

The church, creation of Jesus Christ preserved by the Holy Spirit, has known tensions since its inception. The church, designed to be aggressive as it proceeded from Jerusalem bent on making disciples of all people, has with almost parallel enthusiasm engaged in "civil combat." The "civil war" has always been waged with the noble motive of keeping doctrine pure or purpose in focus. It is always waged (within the Christian Church) in the name of Jesus Christ.

At the church's conception at Caesarea Philippi, Peter, on whose confession the church was built, opened himself to reprimand because he did not understand what it meant for Jesus to be "the Son of the living God." The church was born in the shed blood of God's beloved. Its childhood was tortured by internal stresses as St. Paul's Epistles clearly indicate.

Every heretic martyred in the name of pure doctrine or avowed purpose stands in history as a symbol of a struggle lost or won. Every reformer, and their numbers have been large, is a symbol of convulsive conflict within the church. In the wake of the struggle of "heretics" and reformers the church lies sprawled across history and humanity. It is cracked and splintered into literally thousands of fragments, each fragment waving its own victory pennons. All the pennons together bear muted testimony to the continuing saga of the "civil war" and the fool's gold to which all the things of God transform at the touch of man's finger.

The church today is caught in the throes of these indifferent years. The pangs begin with apostasy, and move through studied apathy, conceptual upheavals, and power struggles. There is great straining to understand these last decades of this millenium. Churchmen grope in near blindness through the struggle and toward the future. Who knows, pressure from the outside may be the very means by which the Holy Spirit brings truce and armistice to the inside. Prayers for the church (not the fragments) are a daily requirement of all God's people in Christ.

A Collect for the Church

Holy Spirit, Lord of the church, whose purpose is to present the church as Bride to Christ the King, and whose task of preparing the Bride for the Bridegroom is mighty and formidable, continue Your great work (with patience for us, who so consistently get in Your way), that the church may be ready for her Lord when He comes to claim her; through Jesus Christ, Your Son, our Lord, with whom You and the Father are one God, with dominion over us forever. Amen.

INTERLUDE
"Thinking"

(Hymn: "God Be in My Head")
Sarum Primer

One of our great gifts from our Creator is the ability to mentally gather facts, then sort, sift, discard, retain, store, recall, examine, and use those facts. Ability to think varies from person to person. Great thinkers have produced great inventions, fashioned almost unbelievable machines, spearheaded great discoveries, and arrived at heroic decisions. The thinking process is exceedingly complicated, as current investigation is discovering. The brain turns off the body in various levels of sleep. At certain of those levels it deals with the previous day's (week's) input, filing, reorganizing, forgetting, sharpening the material that has come to it. Some savants have jumped out of bed with the solution to a problem that had perplexed them for weeks. On the other hand, some, thinking they had sounded new depths, woke in the morning to face the inane thoughts of the night before.

The president of a great computer company allowed time on the job for employees to sit and think. Some wag, using his gray cells, has suggested that everyone ought to take time to "thimk." In recent years thinkers have developed "think tanks," an application of collective minds to knotty problems demanding solutions. The thought process is surely a gift to be treasured, for it is out of the process that civilizations, noble and ignoble, live—and even thoughtfulness issues.

A Collect for the Human Brain

Omniscient God, You gave us brains; give us the brains to use them (in Your service, for our brother, and to our well-being); through Jesus Christ, Your Son, our Lord, with whom You and the Holy Spirit are one God, with dominion over us forever. Amen.

The Gene Pool

(Hymn: "God of Concrete, God of Steel")
Richard G. Jones

Charles Darwin, in agreement with Herbert Spencer's theory of the "survival of the fittest," held that there is in nature a law according to which the fittest alone survive. The stunted and weak plants and animals didn't make it. They were overpowered by the weather, beaten out at meal time in sibling rivalry, or became dinner for a life higher up on the scale. In many animal families the strong dominant male, after asserting and fighting for leadership, sires the young.

The implications were obvious: the plant and animal world have built-in safeguards for the perpetuation of the species. If only the strong could survive in the rugged world of nature, only the best of the genes within the species would be preserved. Man also came under the survival law for most of the years of his existence. In more recent years man has begun to discover ways to shore up "the weak." It is certainly to man's praise that he does. But a new danger faces man, for all human beings contribute to the human gene pool to perpetuate strengths *and* weaknesses. All the human shortcomings which we generally attribute to congenital origins are gene pool problems; conversely, there are a great many gene pool contributions to the "improvement" within the human family as well.

The solutions for the weaknesses do not lie in an "Uebermensch" mentality or in extermination. Certainly restraining by law or by direct surgical intervention is hardly the final answer, although in some cases it may be advisable and gene-pool desirable. If the pool is threatened, it is a problem for the Creator and Preserver of humanity to resolve. While He is working out our destiny, we surely are in order in asking His watchfulness and wisdom for the pool potentials.

A Collect for the Human Gene Pool

Intervene in the spread of defective genes and crippled chromosomes in homo sapiens, great Creator and Preserver of all living things, lest humanity, crown of all creation, weakened by inferior strains in heritage, bring You dishonor and itself disgrace; through Jesus Christ, Your Son, our Lord, with whom You and the Holy Spirit are one God, with dominion over us forever. Amen.

Happy Birthday to the Church
(Pentecost)

(Hymn: "O Where Are Kings and Empires Now")
A. C. Coxe

For all intents and purposes, the Christian church "was born" on the day of the mighty rushing wind and the flames. Appropriately it was on the Biblical festival of Pentecost. Originally the Canaanites, who inhabited the land before the Israelites came, celebrated a harvest festival. God prescribed a similar day for the Israelites when they settled in the land. When the last sheaf of grain had been harvested, there was indeed time for festivity. The day set aside was the 50th day after the Passover. It was a fitting day for the "harvest of souls" who became the first postresurrection Christian community.

The newborn church had for heartbeat the risen and reigning Lord. Its first cry was the proclamation of the power of God's activity in Jesus Christ. It grew by 3,000 souls the first day of its existence. It continued to grow, from Jerusalem, to Judea, and out toward the uttermost parts of the earth.

Through the years it has often thrived with vibrant health; it has many times slumped in depressing sickness. Some feel it reached its zenith in the past; others see its excitement still to come. With all its history, its present status, its future potential, the church is in the direct control of the Holy Spirit. The church is the Bride of Christ, and the Holy Spirit will not present the church to Christ in anything less than perfection.

The church we see is not the church the Spirit sees. The church visible to us is like the jacket covering of a book, which often betrays the story which is inside the covers. To put it another way, we can see only the "visible church," and that is disturbing. The record of the "invisible church" is the true story of the church's years.

A Collect Wishing the Church a "Happy Birthday"

O Holy Spirit of God, whose power and love have nourished and maintained the church for almost two thousand years, may we borrow the Pentecost flames for candles, and the sound of the mighty winds for fanning, not extinguishing them, as we give our blessing to Your church and pray its well-being until the final consummation; through Jesus Christ, Your Son, Our Lord with whom the Father and the Son are one God, with dominion over us forever. Amen!

Words, Words, Words

(Hymn: "Come, O Holy Spirit")
Fred Kaan

There is no argument about it. The gift of words is badly abused. Words are boring to distraction in the mouth of a garrulous friend. They are obnoxious to anger in the hands of an obscene person. They are put together carelessly by the untutored or the careless. They go begging for owners among the illiterate. They exclude the layman from the conversation.

But the gift of words is invaluable. With words the scientist thinks his theories and communicates his discoveries. With words the doctor examines the patient and communicates the sickness he suspects. With words the leader rallies people to his cause. Story tellers hold their readers spellbound. Poets, with beat and rhythm to their words play on the emotions. In measured words the student gains his education; with measured words the essayist develops his thesis; by measured words the mind of man expands.

Every word conveys an idea—"house" for instance, and "in," or "rashly," or "neigh." In the mouth of the dock worker, in the eyes of a student, in the ears of the confessor, in the hands of a poet, words do different things. They illuminate; they educate; they elevate; they damn. If they are sensible and well chosen, they communicate; if they are poorly chosen, they confuse. Their basic function is always the same. They are meant to be a bridge from mind to mind.

Thank God for words, for they build people and nations and churches. And blessed by the power of the Spirit, they populate the mansion prepared by our Lord for those who will hear.

A Collect for Words

Holy Mystery, Wholly Other, unapproachable by any creature in the unfathomable depths in which You dwell, accept our gratitude for the words that reveal Your mighty thoughts and deeds to us, accept our thanks for words that allow us to communicate with each other, and accept our praise for the Word incarnate and regnant, and out of our gratitude let flow a reverence for words, an acceptable use of words, and a filial obedience to the one Word who counts; through Jesus Christ, Your Son, our Lord, with whom You and the Holy Spirit are one God, with dominion over us forever. Amen.

Philosophers

(Hymn: "Immortal, Invisible, God Only Wise")
Walter C. Smith

There is a philological concern for the Christianization of the Greek word *sophia* ("wisdom") that says that "sophia" is of such great dimension it should be used only of God's unfathomable mind. He alone has wisdom in the profoundest and broadest senses of that word. All other thinking, all other wisdom, being inferior to God's, should be labeled, "Philosophia," i.e., love of wisdom. No man can attain to the wisdom of God; the most man can do is search to know the mind of the Lord. It is a high and careful tribute man has paid to the mind of his Creator.

The non-Christian philosopher is humanistic, that is, he works in a system whereby he tries rationally to build out from himself by beginning absolutely by himself. With himself (man) as integration point, he seeks to find all meaning and value. The Christian theologian starts with God, sees man as the holy Word describes him, and begins there. His starting point is God, with man in alienation from God. His search leads him back into the heart and mind of God. The philosopher-humanist continues to search blind alleys. The ancients did well to separate the wisdom of God from the lovers of wisdom.

A Collect for Philosophers

Omniscient Lord, whose Word called light and land and living things into being, and whose hand formed man with consummate skill, guide philosophers away from humanism, which in the end degrades Your creature, to match more nearly Your wisdom which through Jesus Christ raises man to sainthood; through the same Jesus Christ, Your Son, our Lord, with whom You and the Holy Spirit are one God, with dominion over us forever. Amen.

The Critical Balance
of People and Commodities

(Hymn: "O God of Bethel, by Whose Hand")
Philip Doddridge

People-needs for energy are putting great stresses on available supply. Oil to heat homes and run machinery is not unlimited. Conjectures and prognostications see people-needs overbalancing supply within the present generation. It is a terrible thing to have no energy for the furnace, no fuel for transportation, no combustibles to run dynamos. The search for energy has been stepped up. Scientists are looking to the sun, shale, animal and human wastes, the sea—anything that might supply heat and light for the ever-expanding population and the emerging nations.

The balancing act between people-needs and food is even more critical. Not only do the demographical charts vs. food supply threaten future generations, but present population and available grains barely strike a balance. Bring in a flood, or a quake, or unfavorable weather, and hunger to starvation is a real possibility. Enormous shifting of ores and grains between the "have" and "have not" nations goes on. For very conscience' sake no people can deliberately allow another people to die.

A Collect for "Mother Earth"

We do not doubt, O great Creator and Provider, that there is enough resource in the earth to keep the balance between commodity and humanity tipped in man's favor, but give us wisdom enough not to continue exploiting and ravaging it, but rather to exercise good stewardship over it, so that not a single one of us is hungry, or cold, or destitute because of our misguided use of it; through Jesus Christ, Your Son, our Lord, with whom You and the Holy Spirit are one God, with dominion over us forever. Amen.

Meditation at the Guinea Pig Cage

(Hymn: "We Give Thee But Thine Own")
W. W. Howe

The animal houses at research centers are filled with all manner of animal "guinea pigs." Mice, rats, frogs, dogs, monkeys, chickens, guinea pigs, rabbits—to name a few. They bear the burden of a host of illnesses that plague man and animals. It is because of them that behavioral scientists, surgeons, pharmacologists, and others discover causes, search cures, and develop techniques that ultimately serve mankind in its commitment to life and health.

But it is the human "guinea pigs" who ought to come in for some praise and prayer with regularity. They let disease-carrying mosquitoes bite them. They accept experimental vaccines. They submit to new surgical techniques. They swallow pills and placebos, rigidly controlled diets, or nothing at all. They expose their sleep patterns, their timing devices, their sex lives, their body functions, to build charts and chart courses for the human family. Meanwhile, most of us go on our merry way quite oblivious to the risks the human "guinea pigs" take for our well-being. Just now, at least, they are visible. Before they slip back to oblivion, it would be in order to pray for them.

A Collect for Some Heroes

All-wise Lord, whose knowledge encompasses all things in heaven and in the universe, accept our gratitude for all people who put their lives in jeopardy for humanity as the search for weapons to subdue the enemies to our health and well-being goes on; through Jesus Christ, Your Son, our Lord, with whom You and the Holy Spirit are one God, with dominion over us forever. Amen.

Dentists? Dentists

(Hymn: "I Look to Thee in Ev'ry Need")
Samuel Longfellow

Dentistry and dentists have come a long way, thank God. Going to the dentist is not much worse than going to the barber these days. It's time the dentist changed his inevitable sign: "Painless!" to: "Fearless!" We are in an age of dentistry when normal care and correction, at least, are done with a minimum of discomfort.

Connected with dentistry is a veritable host of specialists, from the dental hygienist, through the doctor with the probe, to orthodontists, periodontists, x-ray and lab technicians—all involved with tooth and jaw. The science has come a long way from savage puberty rites that knocked out teeth, and pliers without painkillers, and even from the not-so-long-ago slow-speed drills. Washington wore wooden dentures, and probably looked and felt like it. Today, dentures are so perfected that they not only become part of the wearer, they are even becoming to the wearer. All the dentists' efforts and accomplishments make it possible for all the rest of us to look respectable, feel respectable, smell respectable, and live, as far as mouth-related causes are involved, to a more respectable age. Modern dentistry is more bent on prevention than repair, but today, "repair" is still winning the battle.

A Collect for Dentists

Freely we give thanks to You, Creator God, who fashioned us fearfully and wonderfully, for dentists and all people who repair the damage we do to our mouths in these more decadent days, and as freely we ask You to guide them in their research in preventive dentistry, in their desire to save our teeth, and in their ability to replace them; through Jesus Christ, Your Son, our Lord, with whom You and the Holy Spirit are one God, with dominion over us forever. Amen.

A Christian and His Baptism Are Never Parted

(Hymn: "He That Believes and Is Baptized")
Thomas Kingo

Every person carries his own identifying marks. A mole on his back, the fillings in his teeth, a scar on her leg, help to single each person out from other persons. It is probably true that the same thing applies to animals; else how does a penguin find his mate in the rookery? Crossing over the man/animal barrier presents more problems. To man all sheep look like carbon copies of each other, done in white. Canadian geese seem all cut from the same pattern and colored by the same artist. How they look to each other man will probably never know, but man seeing them in flocks or packs or schools is quite at a loss to tell one from the other.

Man identifies animals in various ways. Birds are caught and banded. Cows are certified with a clip in the ear. Sheep and horses are branded. By bird bands man can record the migration patterns of the species he is interested in. Ear clips mark the cows whose milk has passed inspection. Branding identifies an animal as belonging to a rancher when the time comes to determine to whom the individual sheep or horse belong.

Baptism is many things. It washes away sin, renovates the temple of the Holy Spirit for occupancy, effects a transplant into the body of Christ, confers kingship, brands a lamb, a sheep as God's, and commits the Godhead to a lasting loyalty. Of these exciting baptismal gifts, it is Baptism as the branding of God's lambs and sheep with which we are momentarily concerned. A baptized person bears the mark of God on him. He uniquely through his

Baptism belongs to God. God, of course, does not require brands to identify His sheep. The mark is there for us to realize and remember who we are and to whom we belong. We wear the "brand," the mark (the guarantee of the Holy Spirit), in zephyrs as well as hurricanes, on mountain sides and valleys, in sunshine and in clouds. It can be and is a sustaining truth in our lives.

At the great assize when the sheep and goats are divided, the separating is not done on the basis of brands, but on the basis of faith and commitment. Let him who wears the brand trust not the brand but Christ to whom he belongs when the final decision and division is made.

A Collect for Our Baptism

Prompt us every day, Lord of our lives, to remember our holy Baptism and the privilege, the assurance, the responsibility, and the joy it gives us, for it has made us holy in time and it is our hope for eternal sainthood; through Jesus Christ, Your Son, our Lord, with whom You and the Holy Spirit are one God, with dominion over us forever. Amen.

Notes on Martyrs

(Hymn: "For All Thy Saints in Warfare")
Earl Nelson Horation

Christian martyrs are strangely exciting people. Their excitement is born far less of the manner of their death than the quality of their living. Christian martyrs live with a conviction born of the Spirit that Jesus Christ is Lord. Of such high caliber is their affirmation of this faith, that nothing, man or devil, will turn them from it. Their staunch conviction is prelude to and cause of their martyrdom. Conviction that will face death, and often death by torture, is exciting.

The Old Testament prophets, standing like steel men in the conviction that they bore the burden of a commission from God, met death on the hillsides outside the walls of Jerusalem. Stephen, in the Christian era, met death by stoning. He was the first of a large multitude who would not deny the Christian faith. They were made torches, it is said, to light the gardens of Nero. They were made lion food to satisfy the stranger hunger in the bleachers and box seats of the Roman arenas. They were stoned, crucified, flayed, starved, beaten, exposed.

But martyrs are never victims, for a victim is a passive recipient of his infliction. A martyr faces suffering and death rather than renounce the faith. Know this. The days of Christian martyrs are not ended. Faithful Christians still do and still will suffer and die rather than recant and live. Or, to put it the other way, they will still die and live rather than live to die.

A Collect for All Martyrs

Holy Spirit, Lord of the church, God of the faith and the faithful, we offer our thanks to You for the legions who now carry palm branches in glory, and should we be called to martyrdom, give us hearts strong enough to be martyred for You, thus to add our voice to the cloud of witnesses for time and to the paeans of praise forever echoing through the reaches of glory; through Jesus Christ, our Lord, with whom You and the Father are one God, with dominion over us forever. Amen.

Burdens, Burden Bearers, Burden Sharers

(Hymn: "Within the Maddening Maze of Things")
John G. Whittier

There are burdens, bearers of burdens, and people who share burdens. So many people have burdens. They begin life with them; and then, with the indomitable spirit of mankind, they carry their unique burden to the grave. Others acquire a burden along the way. The system malfunctions, a misstep, an accident—something happens that lays a burden on them. The burden may not be physical. It may be imposed by interpersonal relationships, bad judgment, or ill fortune. Sometimes it can be removed by surgery, by counsel, or by a miraculous answer to prayer. The relief must evoke praise and thanksgiving.

Beside the burden bearers are those who share the burden. Their name is Many. They are the Godsent people who by one means or another make the burden a little less tedious to bear for someone else. Listed among the burden sharers are the empathetic and the sympathetic, parents and siblings, friends and neighbors. Their number includes the professions—the family doctor and gifted surgeon, caseworkers and nurses, neighbors and friends, and all praying people. The sharers contribute a great variety of load-lightening gifts—from a kind and helpful word, through persistence and patience, through know-how and skills.

Strangely, only the recipient of the kind word, the helping hand, or the petitions of a prayer, truly understands how importantly the caring person lightens the burden. If you carry no burden, share another's; you may even, yourself bearing a burden, find strength and love enough to share another's.

A Collect for Burden Bearers

We will probably never understand why some people are born to be burdens, great Creator God, but we can understand that some are born strong and compassionate and some are born to storm Your throne with prayers, so we pray that those born to be loved never realize it, that those born to love have strength to do it, and that those born to pray for the others never fail in their responsibility to them; through Jesus Christ, Your Son, our Lord, with whom You and the Holy Spirit are one God, with dominion over us forever. Amen.

INTERLUDE
A Thought for Underprivileged Children

(Hymn: "Seeing I am Jesus' Lamb")
Henrietta L. von Hayn

Most country kids have endless advantages over most city kids. Living in the country may mean hoeing corn, tending cows, and picking raspberries, but it means barefoot in May, and swimming in the creek, and a chance to get away from the "madding crowd" and be free. Where does the city child go to be alone? Where does he rendezvous with his peers? Can you possibly compare the fire hydrant with an old tire hanging over the old swimmin'-hole?

Childhood only comes once. It ought to be the free and happy time. It has the right of birth to the excitement, dreaming, chattering, serendipitous time. It is the what-shall-I-be-when-I-grow-up time.

City or country, the adult world writes the rules for the next generation's children. The now generation inherited the world created and left to them by the preceding generation; the coming generation inherits the world and the philosophies and the mindsets we impose on them. God preserve us from not making some kind of a positive contribution to today's children, lest they grow up with our faults to be compounded by theirs.

This is not the moment for generalizations. There are children who need T.L.C., which can only be given by another person. Many people are giving great scoops of it as they work with children in youth organizations and community projects for the young fry. We really shouldn't be satisfied that we have done a good job with children until every underprivileged child has received a little love and lifting from the great big adult world. Remember, the task does not begin with George!

A Collect for Underprivileged Children

Divine Creator and Preserver, You created children to be free, and happy, and eager, and excited, and since some have handicaps, of health and parentage, or live in slums and ghettos, and need Your blessing and our help to keep them free and happy and eager and excited, open our hearts to them, that they may have what we can give; through Jesus Christ, Your Son, our Lord, with whom You and the Holy Spirit are one God, with dominion over us forever. Amen.

For Those Who Go Down into Ditches to Work

(Hymn: "Through the Night of Doubt and Sorrow")
Bernard S. Ingemann

They must live in constant fear, they who go down to work in ditches. There are a great many people who work below ground or sea level. The sea has its submariners and the lot of them who work at the ships' boilers. The number increases on the land. Miners of gold, diamonds, and coal climb aboard the de-escalator to descend into the bowels of the earth where for the next eight hours their lives will be at the mercy of the shoring. Tunnelers bore deep into mountains or under bodies of water to make passageways. There are countless ditch diggers who work against the odds of a cave-in and burial before expiration.

Yet their work must go on (in most instances, anyway), for the people must be warmed and the ships must ply the sea and the train must push toward its destination.

Come to think of it, the steelworker, the bridge builder, the ambulance driver, all of us, live in the shadow of that same doom. The difference is in the door frame through which the Grim Reaper elects to come for us.

A Collect for People Who Work in Ditches

Almighty God, You have set us on our course toward conquering and subduing the earth. Be present when men must open it to extract its treasures or to keep pace with civilization's progress, lest they that go into the earth in ditches and deep holes be without divine protection in their dangerous occupations; through Jesus Christ, Your Son, our Lord, with whom You and the Holy Spirit are one God, with dominion over us forever. Amen.

INTERLUDE
Propagating the Kingdoms

(Hymn: "We Would Be Building")
Purd E. Deitz

The kingdom of the world, included theologically in Christ's kingdom of power, grows geometrically in numbers. It's the old game of 2+2=4, 4+4=8, 8+8=16. Before many additions go by, the figures become enormous. It is more alarming if you think that a man and woman marry—that's 2—and have 5 children—that's 7 on the generation overlap or 3 on the population growth tables. If the process happened on the Fibonacci principle, the figures soon enough would go sky high. That principle starts with 1+1, then adds consecutively the last number and the new sum, thus: 1+1=2, 1+2=3; 2+3=5; 3+5=8, and so on. It is on this principle that sunflowers, ram's horns, cowlicks and other devices of nature develop. It is enough to see why the demographers speak of impending S.R.O., the energy people are alarmed, and the food people border on the frantic. But they are not the point of this paragraph. The kingdom of Christ's grace grows by no such geometric principle. It is a face-to-face, one-by-one, muster-courage, speak-the-Gospel, hope-and-pray propagation. It is growth by simple addition. It is growth by adding 1 to the previous total. The addition of each 1 requires the witness, the Word, the hearer, and the Spirit at the = sign or it does not happen. As the Kingdom of Power and the Kingdom of Grace develop in their own ways, the disparity between the two widens with each passing day. With every failure to witness, the disparity grows. The challenge of a Christian world is still staggering. Two thousand years ago the disciples started, with the Pentecost flame in their hearts, to claim the world for Christ. Their witness has brought us in

44

two milleniums to today's ratios. The ratios scream that the challenge to the Christian world is still overwhelming.

A Collect for Heathen, Pagan, Agnostic and Atheist

Since all hope of eternity in glory depends on Christ, our Redeemer, O Lord, grant faith in Him where there is indifference, knowledge and faith where there is ignorance, repentance and faith where unrelieved sin abounds, that all men may have and cherish the eternal hope, and that each may realize its fulfillment in eternity; through Jesus Christ, Your Son, our Lord, with whom You and the Holy Spirit are one God, with dominion over us forever. Amen.

INTERLUDE
Salute to the Men Inbetween
(The Refuse Men)

(Hymn: "Those Who Love and Those Who Labor")
Geoffrey Dearmer

Debris and dust and the wind have buried great cities of the past, often not once but cities at the same site a dozen times. Archeologists sink their shafts and sift the dust searching for the elusive story of past cultures. Today, when the rubbish isn't collected in a big city for a week or so, ghastly mountains grow on the sidewalks. It is not difficult to see why yesterday's cities have become today's archeological digs.

Human refuse today boggles the mind. What if there were no sewers in Paris or garbage collections in Manhattan, or auto dumps in Washington? What if there were no one to empty our waste cans or to devise means to dispose of sewage? Disposing of our debris is a constant job. There are men and women who devote their lives to it!

But imagine the service such people are doing for the rest of us. It isn't just a matter of carting off rubbish or putting sewer crocks into the ground. Every minute they work they are exposed to the bacteria, the germs, the offal that we avoid like poison, even when the mess is our own. Salute such people as these, for they quietly, humbly, amazingly, stand between us and plague at the least, or us and annihilation at worst.

How long would it take a modern city, even with its tall buildings, to become an archeological curiosity of the future if no one did sentry duty at the waste basket!

A Collect for Refuse Men

Great and good God, whose hand stayed the lions' mouths at Babylon, and whose Word guided the leviathan of the sea to Jonah, protect those who establish and maintain our sewage systems from virulent germs, safeguard those who dispose of the daily mountain of our garbage from deadly bacteria, shield those who handle the prodigious piles of our discarded junk from killing viruses, and insulate them against the hurt, the disease and the dying to which they are daily exposed, for in the continual round of their labor they minister mightily to us and bring a needed measure of dignity to Your creation; through Jesus Christ, Your Son, our Lord, with whom You and the Holy Spirit are one God, with dominion over us forever. Amen.

Whatsoever Things Are Beautiful

(Hymn: "The Spacious Firmament on High")
Joseph Addison

Beauty, someone has said, is in the eye of the beholder. That may make Mrs. Umbangi with her six-inch lip discs a beauty for Mr. Umbangi to behold, but it doesn't do very much for Mr. Chin. Mrs. Chin's bound feet (of another year) didn't really do much for Mr. Perry. Beauty is subjective. One lovely lady learned to kiss frogs. Another fell in love with the gentle beast. Not everyone finds warts and nose-bones a joy to behold.

Some things the Umbangis and the Chins and the Perrys must be able to behold and exclaim over in chorus. Surely the "thunder" of a sunrise, the hues of a magnolia tree in blossom, the sunburst of a forsythia bud, or the "flower in a crannied wall" appeal to all of them. What about the crystal waters of a mountain stream, the distant azure mountains, new-fallen snow on a pine forest, and a sky bright with stars?

Beauty is all around us. There is sheer splendor in a child's smile, and wondrous warmth in a mother's touch, and a delightful glow on puppy love. What is more beautiful than a family standing together on a hilltop or grandparents rocking on the porch? Who has not thrilled to the sound of silence on a mountainside or felt the years of living in an old piece of furniture? And spring. And fall.

There are hundreds of other beautiful things. The mystery of mathematics, the gracious heart, a job well done, a gift given or a gift received, friendship, a chord, a phrase of music, and laughter—but the list grows without end.

Things beautiful, tangible and intangible, are a gift of God to be appreciated and cherished. Whoever cannot catch the splendor of beautiful things is impoverished. And who knows, given time, we might even find Mrs. Umbangi beautiful, too.

A Collect for Beauty

Glorious Creator, whose Word called forth all things beautiful and bid them all bring forth after their kind, whose fiat thrust great mountains against the sky and set the stars to singing on their course, accept our gratitude for the joy and wonder Your creation gives to us, and the praise and glory we would add to the paeans all creation lays continually at Your feet; through Jesus Christ, Your Son, our Lord, with whom You and the Holy Spirit are one God, with dominion over us forever. Amen.

On the Optimist

(Hymn: "Rejoice, O People, in the Mounting Years") Albert F. Bayly

Thank God for optimists. He (she) may be betrayed by the weather, beaten in the argument, belittled with an adjective or two, but he stays calm, stays in, checks his facts, rises above the slight, and bounces on to new things. God knows we need people like that.

With the pessimist it is not so. "O dear," he says, "the cup is half gone." Translated, that means something like "Poor me!" or, "Will the rain never stop?" or, "I can't find a good thing to say about him/her/it." With him, no one ever does it right, it's always about to rain, turn cold, or be filled with sea nettles. With him a dark cloud is a dark cloud and no one is about to tell him differently. As a matter of fact, he (or she) gets to be a dark cloud on everyone's horizon, a wet blanket on everyone's party. He even taxes the optimist at times.

For the optimist the word comes differently. "Wow!" he says, "I've still got half a cupful." Translated, that means, "Come now, it's not all that bad!" or, "You mean you really can't see the silver lining on that cloud?" Thank God for optimists; it's good to have a few vocal ones around.

God has sprinkled the world with potential optimists. Anyone who knows himself (females: read "herself") under the dominion of God . . . anyone who knows himself redeemed and the eternal question resolved . . . anyone who knows himself baptized and bearing therefore the guarantee of the Holy Spirit . . . ought to have trouble seeing rain clouds, or sea nettles, or the toad's warts. In the deepest consternation there is always room for "Three cheers for God" from the heart of God's person.

Perhaps we need the pessimists to balance out the optimists, and vice versa. If all the world was pessimistic, who could know an optimist if he saw one? And how would the optimist know he is one without the pessimists who bristle when they see him coming? It is better to be an annoying optimist than a bristly pessimist any day.

A Collect for Optimists

Give to us, gracious and great God, whose vision and love see beyond sin and evil to the human soul involved in it (as so sharply demonstrated by the love of Christ, who "for the joy set before Him endured the cross")— give to us a vision that looks above the half-way mark and a determination to see and know the good in every situation that we may be the bringers of hope and joy to the gloom-spreaders in this good world of Yours; through Jesus Christ, Your Son, our Lord, with whom You and the Holy Spirit are one God, with dominion over us forever. Amen.

On College People

(Hymn: "We Limit Not the Truth of God")
George Rawson

The ancients performed prodigious feats of understanding, planning and building with little more than square, compass, and brute force. Somebody dragged the Stonehenge stones across the fields and set them into position with incredible accuracy. Someone moved the monolithic pillars of the Egyptian temples and the enormous stones of the pyramids down river and built houses for the gods and graves for the pharaohs. Someone discovered the arch, the pendulum, paper, and the printing press. Certainly today's ability to store and retrieve knowledge rivals the invention of the wheel for a place in history.

Keeping some kind of awkward pace with the growing body of knowledge is the school. Once it was enough to learn how to grind flour from Mama and hunting from Papa. Time, holding discovery in its bosom, made its demands on the human mind. Learn to do sums! Learn to read! Learn to draw lines! Learn to solve for x! Once it was enough to do eight grades. A man could make a living with an eighth-grade education. Time and discovery again make new demands. College and university, degree upon degree are required, not only for progress, but just to keep the wheels turning.

No one will ever be master of a subject any more, for the subject has mastered man—and always has. Beyond every frontier of knowledge is the great unknown—and perhaps unknowable. Still, a new batch of young men and women, often in naivete, face the mountain of learning as they start off to school—high, university, graduate. They carry in their starry eyes the hope of man's future, for they will keep knowledge alive and some among them will burst the boundaries that have limited this generation.

"Know the universe I have created," the Creating God implied, and contemporary man seems closer to knowing it than he ever has before. May no man or woman climb the great mountain of knowledge and lose the Creator in the ascent.

Two Collects for God's Blessing on Learners and Learning

Omniscient Lord, You bid us seek out the secrets of Your creation. Guide and bless all who probe the deep mysteries of the universe that their search may always lead to the deeper and divine mysteries, thus satisfying man's need to know Your great universe and Your need for his praise and devotion; through Jesus Christ, Your Son, our Lord, with whom You and the Holy Spirit are one God, with dominion over us forever. Amen.

All-wise God, through whose creative hand man has been fearfully and wondrously made, guide all people by Your power and wisdom to an acceptable stewardship of their bodies, a praiseworthy care and concern for their minds, and a deep appreciation for their redeemed and eternal souls; through Jesus Christ, Your Son, our Lord, with whom You and the Holy Spirit are one God, with dominion over us forever. Amen.

On Behalf of Commuters

(Hymn: "Where Restless Crowds Are Thronging")
Thomas Curtis Clark

The poor commuter, caught in the morning and evening traffic, deserves all the sympathy we can muster. Twice a day, as he moves from suburbia to the inner city, he plays trembling music on his taut nerves. He's in the traffic foray for many hours, inching forward, stopping, starting, standing, perspiring in summer and winter. He's always wondering what's holding up the line, or why the other lane is moving better than his own. After six months, conversation among the poolers is as fickle as the traffic.

It's been like that in the big cities for decades. The narrow roads were their own bottleneck. Now one-way streets and freeways, doubling and tripling the number of cars per square block, add air pollution to the problem. That isn't all. The energy crisis, the possibility of a commuting tax, parking, soaring insurance premiums, to mention a few, add to the consternation. Commuting may be adequately absorbed by daydreamers, but it certainly is no dream world.

From the traffic policeman's helicopter the crawling lanes of traffic look much different. The whole city looks peaceful. None of the ulcer-producing frustrations are present in the cockpit. The lines may move or stand still; from the air they are only lines of cars. An accident on the bridge over the river may have caused a serious back-up problem, but to be removed from it by a thousand vertical feet is to be altogether uninvolved in it. The complicated cloverleaf, a fright to the automobile driver, remind the pilot and announcer of a marble game or a coin sorter. It's all down there. There is no sound or heat or churning stomach to make it real.

If this be the view and the case for the airborne patrolman, however can God know what it is like to be caught in big city traffic? How could Christ who dealt with camels and donkeys and horses possibly understand cars and trucks and crazy drivers? But God did moved into the 20th century with us. And He who is a God afar off (in a helicopter) is a God at hand (with the car pool); or is it the other way around?

A Collect for Commuters

O Lord of infinite patience, give to all who must commute to earn their daily bread, patience, a sense of courtesy, and divine protection; and hasten, O Lord, good solutions to the commuter's mighty problems, lest he be tried beyond endurance and the city die; through Jesus Christ, Your Son, our Lord, with whom You and the Holy Spirit are one God, with dominion over us forever. Amen.

On the Family

(Hymn: "Our Father, by Whose Name")
F. Bland Tucker

Foxes have lairs for their young and the great Canadian goose mates for life. The fearsome grizzly and the lumbering elephant are deeply solicitous of their offspring. The mother hen gathers her chicks under her wings for warmth and a father penguin is an exceptional baby sitter. Whales and porpoises are obviously concerned parents. The blind devotion of the mother sparrow to the gaping jaws of the ugly things that have hatched from her eggs is wonderful.

The animal world's concern for "the family" makes it shattering to see God's highest creation and noblest creature doing less than the birds of the air or the animals of the jungle. Our culture has, in so many instances, disgraced what God meant to be man's greatest joy. Marriageless mating, divorces, abused wives, battered and abandoned children, are cringe material for God and an embarrassment to God's people. The view from the cross must have been horrifying.

The fact that many who have been involved in broken homes, who have abused each other physically and mentally, who have maltreated their children or have been maltreated, think or pray or work themselves into a new and rewarding life is a real joy. The truth that many are too scarred or too scared to come back is a sadness too deep for tears.

It is, conversely, exciting to see people struggling to meet the ideals established by the Lord for the sanctity of the body, or marriage, or home and family. Few things have the same great capacity for evoking warmth and a smile born down deep inside, than a child, and a mother and child, and parents and a child all in love and all at peace. Thank God, families struggling to be families are more numerous than those breaking apart.

A salute is in order this morning for all good mothers, all faithful fathers, and all respectful children. And a prayer must be said invoking the Lord's grace and every blessing upon them and all families.

A Collect for the Family

Eternal God, You have set the solitary in the family, there to be nourished and nurtured, there to be loved and to love. Pour Your grace and peace into all homes, and let Your kind of forgiveness and love, patience and understanding, be practiced in all interrelationships within each family circle; through Jesus Christ, Your Son, our Lord, with whom You and the Holy Spirit are one God, with dominion over us forever. Amen.

INTERLUDE
For All Public Utility Personnel

(Hymn: "Jesus, Thou Divine Companion")
Henry Van Dyke

It is possible to walk through villages in other lands where no public utilities exist. The streets are filthy by day and dark and dangerous by night. People relieve themselves where they are. They burn camel dung in their stoves, sleep with their goats, carry water from a common well, and shield their noses and eyes from the dust with veils. How different our way of life. A flick of a switch and we have illumination flooding the room, turn on an air conditioner, light the stove, flush the toilet, stop the ice maker, get water from a tap, talk anywhere in the world, get the latest news, hear the newest rock, or turn on television. Our car is in the drive; taxi cabs and buses are within hailing distance. Trains and airplanes are almost at our beck and call.

All that service needs minds to contrive it and men to maintain it. How long is it really that telephone service is ever out of order? How much time before the lights come back on? How many days elapse before a temporary bridge is set up after a washout? How long does it take to remove smashed cars and overturned trucks? When was the last time the sewage system failed? How long has it been since the buses or the subway or planes were not at our service?

To keep the city going a multitude of men are out there working, every day, every holiday, every weekend. Electricity, water, gas, and sewage have all ceased to be luxuries. They are a way of life, contrived and maintained by men and women who sweat and strain at their jobs to keep them working for us. Life in some far-off place may be a lot simpler, but who is there who would trade that to which we have become accustomed? The men who climb

58

telephone poles and keep the city dump in working order are worth far more than this little moment of glory and this short prayer!

A Collect for Our Utility People

In these 20th-century years, when our complicated lives depend on complex utility systems, guard, O Lord, the men and women who maintain them in the day to day stresses and dangers of their work, for their sakes, not for ours; through Jesus Christ, Your Son, our Lord, with whom You and the Holy Spirit are one God, with dominion over us forever. Amen.

INTERLUDE
World Hunger

(Hymn: "Thou to Whom the Sick and Dying")
Godfrey Thring

The ability of the towering basketball player or the Oriental juggler to balance a spinning ball on the tip of a finger is fascinating. How tenuously the ball is perched and on how small a pivot point. The Creator has perched this great earth ball as precariously as it spins and wobbles and orbits in its appointed course. As precarious as its orbital balance is, so is the earth's "internal" balance. The polar icecaps determine the ocean levels, the size of continents, the area of tillable land, the population centers, and on and on. Even now the total grain production potential and the population expansion of the earth are on a collision course. Man is always only a summer away from starvation for his food depends on fickle weather patterns. We may be facing the most colossal catastrophe in history. But the truth is 3 billion persons always live in misery beyond the comprehension of Americans. At least a billion people, a third of the world's population, barely make it through the day, so weak are they from hunger. They are open targets for disease and death by starvation. Another billion are on the borderline of malnutrition. The problem of food and feeding is far more complex than shipping our year's abundance to meet another people's pecunery. Politics and education and equipment and money are as much and vastly more a part of the picture and solution as grain-carrying ships. We, as God's people, certainly must be concerned, familiarize, support, and pray for the hungry. Hunger's name is Lazarus, and he lies at every man's gate. The creating and preserving Lord holds our spinning planet and keeps the endless problem of life and death upon it in precarious balance.

A Collect for the Hungry World

Creating and preserving God, whose good providence gives abundance sufficient to satisfy the desire of every living thing, keep us from the foolishness of piling up stores for ourselves but use us as Your instruments to help to feed the hungry and clothe the naked; through Jesus Christ, Your Son, our Lord, with whom You and the Holy Spirit are one God, with dominion over us forever. Amen.

A Collect for the World's Hungry People

Divine Creator, You have bid us be fruitful and multiply. Your blessing multiplies the grain a hundredfold to balance the fruit of the fields with the needs of humanity. Give us charity enough, gifts enough, and know-how enough to move the supply where the demand is, that there be no hungry in our generation; through Jesus Christ, Your Son, our Lord, with whom You and the Holy Spirit are one God, with dominion over us forever. Amen.

For People in Medicine

(Hymn: "Still, Still with Thee")
Harriet Beecher Stowe

The medical field employs great numbers of people and all kinds of skills. Behind the doctor who listens to our hearts with his cold stethoscope and checks our reflexes with his little rubber hammer, stands a backup system second to none. Research people spend lifetimes searching out cures for all that ails mankind. In their search they are led down paths that bring them no results more often than solutions for which they are searching. The X-ray technicians with ever more sophisticated machines probe deeper and deeper into the body, searching for the elusive cause of some poor soul's discomfort. Libraries gather medical information from everywhere in the world and make it available to anyone who asks for it. There is no end to the ramifications of skills and people who make up the medical world.

The decision to become a doctor is no easy choice. The doctor works day in, day out with the hurting, despairing weeping, and dying. He does his very best to effect a cure. He often storms because there is no answer from all the skill and all the libraries and all the research to change the course of a disease sapping the life of a patient. He often weeps in the dark of the night when a patient dies. And if the truth be known, every person in all the backup team weeps with him.

Martin Luther saw everyone who works for the neighbor's well-being as a person "wearing the mask of God." Or, to put it more precisely, God is at work through the men and women who minister to the needs of others, who may therefore be said to be wearing "God's mask." Few doctors or any of the skilled people whose lives are given to the healing arts, deny the divine behind the human, a Creator behind the creature, God's intervention for better or worse (as we see it) in the health and sickness of man. God's being there affects the content of any prayer for the medical world.

A Collect for the People in Medicine

Great Creator, whose will for the well-being of people shone through every healing miracle of Jesus, Your Son, bless all who are involved in the ministry of healing with knowledge and wisdom, courage and strength, and through them touch the lives of all whose health is ailing or failing, that the sick may be whole and the dying given life, to Your praise and honor; through Jesus Christ, Your Son, our Lord, with whom You and the Holy Spirit are one God, with dominion over us forever. Amen.

INTERLUDE
On Silence

(Hymn: "Breathe on Me, Breath of God")
Edwin Hatch

Never underestimate the value of silence. True, silence can be overwhelming as it is in the reaches far from civilization. It can be debilitating as sometimes it is for those who live deep in a snowbound Norwegian fjord. These are the exceptions. Silence has its own values and makes its own contribution to him who seeks it and to him who uses it.

Solomon is said to have built his temple without the sounds of hammers. "Silence," someone has said, "is the tribute Solomon's workmen paid to God." Isaiah had a word on silence: "In quietness and confidence shall be your strength!" St. Paul wrote of it once when he bid the Thessalonians: "Study to be quiet." A marginal reference to the "still, small wind," in which God came to Elijah, is "a voice of gentle stillness."

We do terrible things to silence. We fill it with voices, shattering it sometimes with a whisper. We fill it with music, loud and raucous, soothing and gentle, and it is no longer silence but music. We keep the television on low to keep us company, the stereo running so we don't have to think, the radio playing to cover a void. Each instrument absorbs the silence and leaves behind its own poor substitute.

Silence, like a rest in music, offers life an opportunity to catch up or the soul an opportunity to anticipate. Silence allows deep thinking and earnest praying. Silence gives God a chance to speak and man a chance to hear Him.

Not all silence is creative. An unanswered cry for help is frightening. A dungeon from which all sound has been eliminated has its own terror. Deafness, the awful ailment that eliminates because it denies communication, brings only loneliness with it.

But the other silence, the creative silence, the silence that allows the voice of God to be heard—that's special!

A Collect on Silence

Divine Creator, as You lived in the awesome silence of eternity, and broke it at last with the thunder of primeval chaos, with the singing of the morning stars, and the song of gentle thrushes on the wing, so let us keep silence on occasion; so let Your nearness be known and Your voice of gentle stillness be heard; so let holy praise and divine purpose issue from it—and peace, and hope, and confidence; through Jesus Christ, Your Son, our Lord, with whom You and the Holy Spirit are one God, with dominion over us forever. Amen.

INTERLUDE
On Work

(Hymn: "Behold Us, Lord, a Little Space")
John Ellerton

To promise your lady love that all she need worry about if only she will say, "Yes," is that she will "sit on a cushion and sew a fine seam," sounds fine. It also sounds monotonous. And it sounds as if a "hothouse flower" is about to be born. What's the matter with work? Work, physical or mental, is good for the whole person. Genesis 4 mixed up many people with its threatening, "by the sweat of your brow" existence.

There is a lot of laziness around. People are all too willing to let George do it. The number of market baskets in the parking lot, the rubbish on the roadside, the unkempt empty lot in the city block, are quiet and persistent reminders of the lazy among us. The mess in the meeting hall, the cigarette butts on the marble floors, the condition of public washrooms are an almost unforgiveable indictment of John Q. Public.

Everyone must work to live . . . or leech. Wondrously, the very rich often work enormous hours for the common good. There are many who "hate" the work they have to do or who must work under adverse conditions. There are, fortunately, as many who enjoy the work, and count themselves blessed for the satisfaction it brings them. Many work hard and retire early; and of these another many give themselves freely to volunteer work, lending the helping hand that makes institutions—hospitals, nursing homes, churches—possible. What a shame that there are those who can actually "sit on a pillow," living out their days in a ceaseless round of uselessness.

Orchids to those who are not afraid of work, pleasant or unpleasant. Salutations to those who seek work to be done and do it. Quiet praise to all who accept a job because they are asked. Faint praise to those who work and grumble while doing it. No praise to those who work only for hire. Shame on those who can and will not work.

A Collect for Work

O Son of God, who came to minister rather than to be ministered to, and who sanctified work by soiling Your hands to do it, give us willingness, strength, and love that we may with joy add to the well-being of each of the communities of which we are a part by our ready and willing service to them; who with the Father and the Holy Spirit are one God, with dominion over us forever. Amen.

Pity the Poor Policeman!

(Hymn: "My Country, 'Tis of Thee")
Samuel F. Smith

Pity the poor policeman, whatever the uniform he wears. His task is not the easiest; the support he gets is not the strongest. If he is a traffic "cop" at a downtown intersection, fenders miss him by inches time and time again. He breathes the polluted air of the city. If he walks a beat he has potential hazards at every corner and flirts with maiming and death at every step. If he rides a squad car he is on call, never knowing what the next crackling shortwave summons may bring: a bloody accident, a "shoot-it-out" robbery, a life-risking chase through the city, or a question about direction.

His job is as unpopular as any job can be. He writes tickets. He reprimands. He arrests. He testifies in court. He's the man in the white hat and on the other side in far too many people's minds. People avoid him. They give him a wide berth. They are afraid of him. He lives with his feeling, they live with theirs. Too often the two don't meet.

What it takes the courts leisurely weeks to do, the lawman must do in a split second. To ticket or not to ticket, to arrest or not to arrest, to charge or not to charge, to shoot or not to shoot . . . blessed if he does, cursed if he doesn't, and, in almost every instance, vice-versa. Then, in court, he testifies and the judge rules against his decision.

His is a job that society makes necessary. As long as people are people and sin is sin, he will have to be there. The quiet tragedy of the whole task is that he gets such faint praise for risking his life every day to keep the village, the town, the city, the country, a reasonably safe place in which to live. People who enforce the law need our prayers!

A Collect for Our Lawmen

God of authority and justice, whose concern extends to law and order in the land, bless and protect all people who daily hazard their lives to uphold the law and to maintain order among us; through Jesus Christ, Your Son, our Lord, with whom You and the Spirit are one God, with dominion over us forever. Amen.

The Gospel of Peace

(Hymn: "Thy Kingdom Come, O Lord")
Frederick L. Hosmer

It is absolutely paradoxical. On the one hand stands the Gospel of Peace. On the other hand stands the world, unclaimed, untamed. Here is the Prince of Peace; there is the god of war and violence, astride the nations and reveling in the adulation of the violent ones. Christ lives in the hearts of His people, but He has been too often locked in an attic room. It is not hard to understand some godless leader pillaging, ravaging, and murdering. It is incomprehensible that the man of God can worship and curse with the same lips, offer alms and brutality with the same hands, or think on "whatsoever things are pure" and hate with the same mind. Yet the Spaniards, bearing crosses, killed South Sea Islanders for sport and Aztecs for gold. The French knights, moving to wrest the Holy Land from the Turks, their shields adorned with holy symbols, often behaved themselves more like Ghengis Khan than men of God. We are a Christian country. We have acquitted ourselves with nobility in countless ways. Yet in the name of freedom of religion we murdered Indians and in the name of economics we tyrannized a race. In the name of unity we have slain our thousands. In the name of Christ the church would do well to love the world enough to proclaim Christ's kind of peace. She cannot stop until all mankind calls Him Lord and the lamb lies down with the lion and the nations know war no longer, and the violent know peace.

A Collect for Peace

Almighty Father, whose angels sang of peace at the advent of Your Son, and who sacrificed that same Son

to validate the angelic proclamation, spread the
glorious word of reconciliation in Jesus Christ, the
Savior, with great dispatch to every corner of the world
where humanity has not learned it, beginning with and
through me, and forgive those in our family who
struggle so for supremacy over others at such awesome
prices; through Jesus Christ, Your Son, our Lord, with
whom You and the Holy Spirit are one God, with
dominion over us forever. Amen.

Mission Activity at Home

(Hymn: "Hope of the World")
Georgia Harkness

A frightening possibility confronts the Christian church each year of its existence. In one year or one generation, the Christian church could cease to exist. Supposing no one bothered to speak the Word with its inherent power of the Holy Spirit to convict and convince. Before long we would have an American version of the Russian Museum of Atheism and Religion in Leningrad, right here in Washington. Curious people could move from display case to wall hangings, wondering about the strange gold cups, the unusual and meaningless banners, and the peculiar clothing some people used to wear. "What's that cross all about," they might ask and laugh with the attendant at his flip answer. We are a year, a generation, from the other possibility as well. What would happen if every Christian "screwed his courage to the sticking point" and witnessed to the Christ within him? And what if he backed up his words with prayer and his prayer with a Christlike life? And if he took his Bible seriously enough to study it and meditate on it "day and night"? So gentle is the pressure we exert that it takes a whole congregation—500 or 600 strong—to bring in one, maybe two, converts a year. It is high time purposes and pressures and prayers and words and life and living be stepped up. Charity begins at home. So does the delivery of the Good News of Jesus Christ to the community.

A Collect for Missions

Eternal Father, who sent Your Son to redeem our sinful world, who in turn has commanded us to be in mission to the world, forgive all indifference in us that allows any fellow man to die without a confrontation with Christ, and make and keep us always mindful of our sent-ness, to the glory of Your kingdom and the honor of Your name; through Jesus Christ, Your Son, our Lord, with whom You and the Holy Spirit are one God, with dominion over us forever. Amen.

On a Special Breed of People

(Hymn: "O Perfect Love")
Dorothy F. Gurney

The words from the wedding ceremony "till death us do part," are lived out in most noble commitment and quiet splendor in a hundred places. Just now those marriages that move to high number anniversaries with little or no effort are not in question. It is those marriages where the commitment to love ought, by the vicissitudes within them, to break and don't, that are. Three cheers and a hearty "Hurrah," followed by a terribly sincere "God bless you, noble man or noble woman!"

John was a man like that. Judith's arthritis crippled her beyond almost any movement. John turned her over in bed at night. He fed her every spoonful of food she ate and every drop of water she drank. He dressed and undressed her. All the while he said cheery things to her, hope things, buoying things. Day after relentless day. "Until death you do part?" the minister asked him. "Until death us do part!" was not, in the end, what really maintained his commitment; it was deep, still, wonderful love that gave without asking. It's good to know that they are in glory now. Her hands, her back, her legs, are straight again. They surely walk the streets where Jesus is with joy.

John is for the moment every man and woman who is doing the "John" kind of loving, and Judy is every woman and man who must by life's often outrageous fortune be waited on and nursed and loved "until death us do part." Such great people are a reproach to the flippant committed only to themselves. They are a superb example of what it means to be committed to an ideal and to loving. What a sadness that the patient loving goes on and the world goes by unheeding.

A Collect for the Trembling Sparrows

Great and gracious Lord, whose concern for a falling sparrow and the hair count on any given head is notorious since the days of Christ's visit, grant strength and patience, kindness and love to all who tend the trembling infirm, and to the falling sparrows, O Lord, give Your tenderest blessing that each may know You know and care; through Jesus Christ, our Lord, who with the Father and the Holy Spirit are one Lord with dominion over us forever. Amen.

A Prayer for the Seedtime
(A Springtime Devotion)

(Hymn: "With Songs and Honors Sounding Loud")
Isaac Watts

How we must try our God's patience! We do wonders with preventive medicine, preventive dentistry, preventive maintenance. We haven't done very well with preventive prayer. We have a real capacity for making prayer retroactive. We summon God to change yesterday's course.

The problem is good weather for the picnic. The day dawns dreary with a 90 percent chance of rain. "Please, God!" But the rain cloud started its nefarious course eight days before the picnic date. For eight days it was on a collision course with Middle Town. Of course, the great Stiller of Storms could stay the raindrops, but the decision was made days ago.

City folk get around to praying for the seeds at Thanksgiving time. By that time God has blessed the seed, the planting, the growing, and even the harvest. If He had waited for the city folk, they would have begun scrounging for seed about the time they should have been harvesting.

Country folk know better. Their bread and butter depends on the seed going in at its appointed time. Fortunately, they are praying for the harvest long before it arrives, for the harvest always depends on the seedtime— and the tilling, and the rain (that spoiled the picnic), and the sunshine.

But then, perhaps it works itself out properly after all. The great sowing and harvesting machinery, the great moving equipment, and a host of farmer needs are city-conceived and city-born. The men who make the machines must eat. The prayer begun by the fervent petitions of the farmers in the seedtime concludes with the fervent thanksgiving of the machinists in the fall. By their prayers both farmer and machinist, in petition and thanksgiving, acknowledge their dependence on the creating and preserving Lord.

A Collect for the Seedtime

Benevolent God, whose universal grace supplies the needs of all living things, bless the plowing, the seeding, the weather, the growing, that the earth may yield a hundredfold, and the harvest be indeed a time for rejoicing because the desires of every living thing are satisfied; through Jesus Christ, Your Son, our Lord, with whom You and the Holy Spirit are one God, with dominion over us forever. Amen.

Laughter Is a Great Gift

(Hymn: "In Thee Is Gladness")
Johann Lindemann

Laughter is such a gift. Not the sneering laugh of the archvillain or the hellish laugh of Satan. Not the judging Lord "holding them in derision," either. But, from the smile that betrays a laughing heart to the great belly laughs, laughter is a gift.

It is a privilege to laugh "about" some wondrous incident with an unexpected twist. It is an equal privilege to laugh with family and friends at some shared memory or well-turned joke. Such laughter has a way of drawing those who share it into a common bond, however fleeting.

Of course, laughter can be a terrible thing when it is done in scorn. It can be a sinful thing if it is evoked by some evil premise. The laugh-evoker and the laugher must always be guarding their ground, for both are guardians of the premise.

But there are people with the wondrous capacity to make people laugh. They have the capacity to build the story, to make the gestures, to hold the suspense until the precise moment. More power to them!

Pity the people who are not able to laugh, to whom nothing is funny. They never opened the gift and are thus deprived of one of life's fine blessings. Pity, too, the people who are laughed at, for laughter that takes its toll from another person is cruel and thoughtless. And pity the person who finds his humor at the expense of another.

It is good to know that God appreciates laughter. Tucked here and there in the Scriptures are some neat notes about it. "A merry heart maketh a cheerful countenance," it notes. Or, "He that is of a merry heart hath a continual feast," and, "A merry heart doeth good like a medicine."

A Collect for Laughter

We appreciate and say our gratitude for the ability to laugh, for the people who make us laugh, and for the people who laugh at our humor, and we ask that You keep alive in us in all places, at all times, and in all things, the capacity to smile and even to laugh, O great and majestic God, who yet and ever loves the merry heart; through Jesus Christ, Your Son, our Lord, with whom You and the Holy Spirit are one God, with dominion over us forever. Amen.

INTERLUDE

Notes on Motherhood
(Mother's Day)

(Hymn: "Children of the Heav'nly Father")
Caroline V. S. Berg

Children are gifts of God to parents, though sometimes neither parents nor children believe it. Fathers, too often, exercise their half of the miracle of procreation—and disappear. Mothers as often exercise their portion of the miracle—and find themselves with child. What a pity that some people conceive and rebel, and that those who are conceived live to resent it. The blame, even in ill-conceived situations, cannot be laid at the feet of our Lord. He not only gave us the capacity, but free will. Whatever reins He set to procreation are found in the Decalog or in the two-pronged love command, "Thou shalt love the Lord thy God; Thou shalt love thy neighbor."

There is bad news and good news. Let's continue with the bad news to get that out of the way. What are the aborted fetuses, abandoned babies, battered children, illegitimate sons and daughters, belabored youths, and disowned delinquents doing this Mother's Day? What are the fathers and mothers, whose shelter and love, and goals, and hopes, and mores, and morals, and forgiving and praying are defied by their children, doing today? And what are the mothers (and fathers) whose infant hopes became burdens, demanding enormous material prices, high time prices, great energy drains, and at the end emptiness and relief and sadness, doing today?

There is good news. A salute to mothers (and fathers) who understand their God-given role, who tenderly, lovingly, with great concern assumed the responsibility with joy, and trembling, and prayer! A salute to children who are the pride of their parents, not because of their achievements but because of integrity! A prayer for those whose burden is heavy, who pray in the night and weep in the darkness, who wait at the front stoop for a son or a daughter to come home!

Aye! Mothers and fathers need a word of thanks and a word of hope and a word of praise. For so many of them, one day set aside for them is simply not enough. Every day is family day.

A Collect for the Generations

God, almighty yet gracious, Father of all mankind, who set the stars to singing and placed the solitary in the family, make us grateful and empathetic for our progenitors and give us wisdom, patience, forgiveness, and love for the generation You gave to us; through Jesus Christ, Your Son, our Lord, with whom You and the Holy Spirit are one God, with dominion over us forever. Amen.

On Behalf of the Military

(Hymn: "O Day of God, Draw Nigh")
R/B. Y. Scott

"A strong man armed keeps his goods in peace." In the kingdom of power it is power that controls. Let a nation become starry-eyed and it will soon have "weary eyelids closed in death." No nation can afford to sit on its laurels or to trust in the inherent goodness of men. The alert nation, the armed nation, the nation committed to survival stands a chance at survival. Lesser, ill-prepared nations have folded before the march of the Hittites, of Alexander the Great, of the mighty Caesars, of Attila, of the Moslems. The biggest threat to our nation in this century is Communism.

Communism has waved its big stick and announced to the world that one day it intends to rule it all. October 1917—revolution in Russia. 1949—takeover in Red China! Then the 20th-century march: Roumania! Bulgaria! Hungary! Poland! Estonia! Latvia! Czechoslovakia! Mongolia! Tibet! Vietnam! Cambodia! Cuba! It is making inroads into Italy, France, Spain, Germany.

The killing capacity of the great nations has become the power to overkill. Spying is done by satellite. A phone call at the Kremlin or from the Oval Office could perpetrate a holocaust. Weapon destruction and weapon delivery is accurate to inside the ellipse at Washington or Red Square in Moscow. The powers balance precariously these days. Uneasy lie the heads of millions upon millions of people throughout the whole world.

Government operates in the kingdom of power. Nygren has called the area in which the nations move (in his Romans commentary) the aeon of darkness. In the darkness the powers face each other without trust. The military of our land must be maintained or we perish! The kingdom and the aeon are like that. As long as the military must continue, as long as the world lasts, the church, living in it, must be involved in it. The military needs the concern of the church. Our prayers, our contributions of substance or of self, are Christian concerns, too, to "keep the goods in peace." It is in the Kingdom of Grace we do our praying; in the kingdom of power every citizen may have to stand ready to do battle to the death to "keep the goods" at all.

A Collect for the Military

Omnipotent God, who in the ancient garden watched Satan drive wedges between our first parents, between them and You, and through all the years since, between all people, guard all those committed to the necessity of the defense of our good land and hasten the promised peace that Christ brings between people and You, between people, and between peoples and so fulfill Your ancient and continuing will; through Jesus Christ, Your Son, our Peace, with whom You and the Holy Spirit are one God, with dominion over us forever. Amen.

INTERLUDE
Tuning In on the Media

(Hymn: "Christ for the World We Sing")
Samuel Wolcott

In the first quarter of the 20th century invisible air waves began to carry sound. People stretched an aerial from the barn to the house (or used the bedsprings, which worked just as well), wound wire around an oatmeal box, ran impulses through a galena, attached earphones and listened to the President, a symphony—and advertising. Radio techniques grew steadily through loudspeakers, cabinets, FM, and stereo. Now people talk from car to truck driver on the citizens' band, from nation to nation via satellite.

In the second quarter of the century pictures were added to sound. The vacuum tube, lying around for several decades without application, came into its own! At first the pictures were black and white and small. They were enlarged with great magnifying glasses sliding in grooves for adjustment in front of the screen.

Color was added in the third quarter, first falteringly, then in locked-in brilliance. And of course, advertising continued to pay for the free entertainment and the free education the public was getting through the tube. Families which began with one television set have grown up into three-television-set people to avoid the one-set struggle of who gets to choose the channel.

It is all a deep mystery—that people can walk about with all that talking and music and color zinging through them and not feel a thing!

It is to the church's credit that she got on the wagon early in the radio development and at the outset of the television era. Her mission is to proclaim the Gospel of Jesus Christ. She was quick to see the possibilities of

84

reaching unreachable people by coming into their dens and sickrooms at the flick of a channel selector. God alone knows the "savings," the "comfortings," the "life changings" that have occurred because of those who were concerned enough "to send the very best" by air.

A Collect for the Mass Media

Almighty and gracious God, You have done so many and such great things for us and have bid us proclaim salvation through the cross. Bless the efforts of Your church as it uses the mass media for the proclamation of Your awesome Law and saving Gospel for the temporal and eternal well-being of every living person; through Jesus Christ, Your Son, our Lord, with whom You and the Holy Spirit are one God, with dominion over us forever. Amen.

Contrast to Triumph
(Palm Sunday)

(Hymn: "Angels of the Heav'nly Father")
O. Wm. Luecke

The sounds of Palm Sunday are absolutely triumphant. Triumph filled the narrow Jerusalem streets when He rode in on that little donkey. "Hosanna!" they cried, and, "Blessed is He that cometh!" and, "Hosanna to the Son of David!" What with all the palm branches strewn on the cobble pavement it was absolutely the equivalent of a 20th-century ticker-tape parade. The people doffing shawls and sashes, and spreading them in the dirty street, anticipated by two millennia the red carpet treatment.

St. Luke, under the Holy Spirit's inspiration, of course, makes an editorial comment on the spontaneity of the palm parade. As far as he was concerned the crowds weren't there in praise of Christ. They hoped to see some miracle done. With a little phrase between two commas, Luke takes the wind out of all the Hosannas. The people shouted their adoration of Jesus who could feed five thousand men (not to mention the women and children who might have been there) with a little boy's lunch.

Once the cross was done and the grave empty, it became possible to put Hosanna back into "Hosanna!" The cross and grave have removed the scales from people's eyes so that they might see the Christ who comes. The old tension (that must have had its own unique terror for Jesus) is gone. We can, we do, shout our Hosannas and blow our trumpets and wave our palm branches because Jesus is Lord, our Lord.

In the midst of all the shouting why not a contrast? Why not a gentle word about the wonder of God's holy angels who praise Him night and day? We do need His angels, you know. Sometimes in our big adult way we slough off the whole idea of angels. "They are great for children, but not for me." But who wants to get too big for angels? Do we really get too big to need them, we who are the children of God?

From bread and fish to angels is something less than a millimeter. For the sake of angels we could be standing alongside Luke's Palm Sunday crowd! Whether bread or the messengers of God—if it is Christ, the Son of the living God, who gives them to you, there is God-pleasing content to your Palm Sunday praise.

A Collect for the Lord's Watching

Eternal God, whose hand holds steady beneath us, whose wings shield us in the storms, and whose heart warms us with such great concern, keep us and all Your children conscious of and trusting in Your might and mercy, Your care and love, lest we falter on the waves or find the chill beyond Your tender care; through Jesus Christ, Your Son, our Lord, with whom You and the Holy Spirit are one God, with dominion over us forever. Amen.

Affirming the Resurrection
(Easter Day)

(Hymn: "For All the Saints")
William W. Howe

Jesus, the Christ, is the first fruit of the resurrection from the dead. To use an anthropomorphical picture, the great Father God reached into the dark of the cave where the still body of Jesus had been laid to rest. Those who had put Him there had done all the proper things that time allowed between His death and sunset. They cried, for they knew that from death there was no return, and their Friend and Champion was very dead. Grave covers and hillsides do not hinder God. He reached into the cave and touched Jesus.

Vivit! He lives!

He emerges from the grave. (He leaves the rolling away of the stone and straightening of the winding sheets to the angels.)

He demonstrates His resurrection to His friends and followers.

He ascends.

He sits at the right hand of the Father.

He rules.

And after Him ascend the hosts of the faithful, who in life found Him Savior and Lord, who now, in death, find Him their resurrection and new life. They follow to fill the mansions, to bring the population of heaven to its present levels. They stand in the glory place around the great throne. They chant the descant to the Lamb they learned so long ago. "Blessing and honor and glory and power be unto Him," they chant. Heaven is richer because they are there.

We are rich knowing they are there, too. Death is not annihilation after all. Death is life! Those who die in the Lord are with Him for eternity. Weep not for those who die in Christ. They have only just gone home.

A Collect for Those in Glory

Eternal Father, who since eternity has been willing to share heaven with us mortals for all eternity, accept our profoundest gratitude for all the saints who, even as we are praying, see the shining face of Jesus and sing the glory songs for Him and maintain us in the faith-relation with Jesus Christ, that we may join them when at last our hour comes; through the same Jesus Christ, Your Son, our Lord, with whom You and the Holy Spirit are one God, with dominion over us forever. Amen.

INTERLUDE
On Being the Middle Man
(Stewardship)

(Hymn: "Son of God, Eternal Savior")
Somerset C. Lowry

One of the best things about croquet is the occasional right to place your ball alongside your opponent's and hit your ball with your mallet. The kinetic energy, transferred from the mallet, through your ball to his, sends his ball scooting out of the court. Someone made a mint out of the idea years ago by suspending six or seven steel balls in a row. The end ball, lifted and freed, swung into the one adjacent to it. Energy passed through the in-between balls, and sent the ball on the other end swinging out on its string. The energy passed from one end ball back and forth, until it was all used up.

All of which is meant to get at the whole idea of stewardship. Like the croquet mallet or the end steel ball, our Lord has literally released great power against us. Chalk off the list: body, soul, eyes, ears, my reason and all my senses; also clothing, shoes, meat and drink, house and home, and all my goods. Add provision, protection. Add redemption from death and the power of the devil. Add election to grace, sanctification, hope and heaven. And everyone knows a list like that is far from complete! God's gifts are stored-up energy. They are motivating force. They are the first principle of stewardship!

After a "hit" like that, what manner of people God's people ought to be! "Yes, Lord" to the death is barely enough gratitude. "Yes" to the Beatitudes, "Yes" to being salt and light. "Yes" to loving God and neighbor. "Yes" to the Ten Commandments. "Yes" to using talents. "Yes" to tithing. "Yes" to committees and meetings and helping and giving. "Yes" to burning out for God.

90

Of the two above illustrations, the first is the more valid. Those static center steel balls might suggest that you just stand there and let George do it, which isn't what God meant at all.

A Collect for Stewards

Creator God, to whom all the forces of the universe belong, and who gives to our care and ownership a goodly portion of them, bless us with all we need to support our families and ourselves, guide us in a careful stewardship of our blessings, and thus maintain Your kingdom among us and in the world; for the sake of Jesus Christ, Your Son, our King, with whom You and the Holy Spirit are one God, with dominion over us forever. Amen.

INTERLUDE
The Church in Mission

(Hymn: "Lord, We Thank Thee for Our Brothers")
Roger K. Powell

The church, the sum total of all committed to the blessed Trinity, lives in obedience to her Lord. Or she ought to! She owes her existence to Him. She is nourished by Him. Her hopes derive from Him. How could she do otherwise?

Her Lord has set her on her mission. He has spelled out her purposes. He has given her the blessing of the Holy Spirit. Hers to be in mission, carrying out His purposes, knowing that the blessing of the Holy Spirit gives the increase.

To His church the Lord has given the responsibility of calling men to repentance, that is, to take the 180° turn from whatever gods they may be worshiping to the worship of the living God. To that end, the church is to herald the Gospel, that is, the saving news of Jesus Christ. "Go!"

The church is to imitate its Lord. The Matthew "Inasmuch"-parable sets the pattern of sacrifical love for the endless line of people in need. The church must see in every pauper, in every prisoner, in every ailing human being, the face of her Lord. "Serve!"

The Lord's command, "Love thy neighbor as thyself," is a command to the church. Her love must extend to herself. She must constantly look to her wounds, her fragmentation, her self-serving, for she is best when she is hale.

Hers is the responsibility of learning and teaching. She must teach herself, lest she grow stagnant for want of learning; she must teach all who will listen. It is wrong for her to believe that she has all knowledge; it is wrong for her

92

to think that the mystery can be solved without its being revealed.

The church, sum total of all committed people, lives in obedience to her Lord. You are the church! Are you the church?

A Collect for the Mission of the Church

Jesus, our Lord, who prayed in the upper room that we might be one, who on the cross prayed that the eternal Judge hold back the damnation of our sinful world, and who groans in prayer for us even now as our Mediator and Advocate, hear our prayer—that we may not be guilty of thwarting Your dream of unity and peace, that the trumpets set to signal judgment day stay silent, and that the holy mission of Your Kingdom capture us in order that all men may know You, and come to the knowledge of Your truth; who with the Father and the Holy Spirit are one God, with dominion over us forever. Amen.

Sources of Hymns Suggested for Interludes

BWUSF Book of Worship for U.S. Forces
PH Pilgrim Hymnal (Pilgrim Press, Philadelphia)
PP Pilgrim Praise (Galliard, England)
SBH Service Book and Hymnal (Augsburg, Fortress)
SSH Sunday-School Hymnal (Concordia)
TLH The Lutheran Hymnal (Concordia)
WS Worship Supplement (Concordia)

Angels of the Heav'nly Father	Source unknown
Behold Us, Lord, a Little Space	*PH* 395
Breathe on Me, Breath of God	*PH* 233
Children of the Heav'nly Father	*SBH* 572
Christ for the World We Sing	*PH* 295
Come, O Holy Spirit	*PP* 22
Day of Wrath, O Day of Mourning	*TLH* 607
For All the Saints	*TLH* 463
For the Beauty of the Earth	*PH* 66
From All Thy Saints in Warfare	*WS* 756
God Be in My Head	*PH* 543
God of Concrete, God of Steel	*BWUSF* 72
He That Believes and Is Baptized	*TLH* 301
Hope of the World	*PH* 398
I Look to Thee in Ev'ry Need	*SBH* 490
Immortal, Invisible, God Only Wise	*WS* 769
In Thee Is Gladness	*WS* 768
Jesus, Thou Divine Companion	*PH* 409
Jesus, with Thy Church Abide	*PH* 301
Lead Me, Lord	*PH* 524
Lord, We Thank Thee for Our Brothers	*PH* 268
My Country, 'Tis of Thee	*PH* 437
Not Alone for Mighty Empire	*SBH* 345

O Day of God, Draw Nigh	*PH* 444
O God of Bethel, by Whose Hand	*SBH* 516
O Perfect Love	*TLH* 623
O Where Are Kings and Empires Now	*SBH* 154
Our Father, by Whose Name	*PH* 466
Rejoice, O People, in the Mounting Years	*PH* 304
Seeing I Am Jesus' Lamb	*SSH* 242
Son of God, Eternal Savior	*PH* 413
Still, Still with Thee	*SSH* 39
The Spacious Firmament on High	*PH* 72
Those Who Love and Those Who Labor	*PH* 403
Thou to Whom the Sick and Dying	*SBH* 464
Through the Night of Doubt and Sorrow	*SBH* 329
Thy Kingdom Come, O Lord	*PH* 118
Thy Hand, O God, Has Guided	*SBH* 159
We Give Thee But Thine Own	*TLH* 441
We Limit Not the Truth of God	*PH* 259
We Would Be Building	*PH* 494
Where Cross the Crowded Ways of Life	*PH* 423
Where Restless Crowds Are Thronging	*SBH* 355
With Songs and Honors Sounding Loud	*PH* 459
Within the Maddening Maze of Things	*PH* 360